Part 4

Student
Activity
Book 4

PEARSON

Scott
Foresman

scottforesman.com

Editorial Offices: Glenview, Illinois • Parsippany, New Jersey • New York, New York
Sales Offices: Boston, Massachusetts • Duluth, Georgia • Glenview, Illinois
Coppell, Texas • Sacramento, California • Mesa, Arizona

ISBN: 0-328-26053-3

11 12 13 14 V001 15 14 13 12 11

Table of Contents

I am Diz.

Picture Page

Picture Page **Lesson 97**

Activity 5

Writer's Warm-Up

k   k

k   k

z   y

e   w

j   u

h

Name _____

Rescue the Cat

_____
- - - - - - - - - - - - - - - - -
_____

_____
- - - - - - - - - - - - - - - - -

_____
- - - - - - - - - - - - - - - - -

_____
- - - - - - - - - - - - - - - - -

_____
- - - - - - - - - - - - - - - - -

Activity 8

8

Sentence Page

Sentence Page   Lesson 98

I   am   Nat.

Activity 4

9

Picture Page

Activity 4

Writer's Warm-Up

Name _____

Sentence Page

Sentence Page Lesson 99

Nat can hop.

Activity 4

13

Picture Page

Picture Page   Lesson 99

Sentence Page

Diz | can | not | hop.

Name _____

Picture Page

Picture Page Lesson 100

Writer's Warm-Up

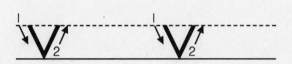

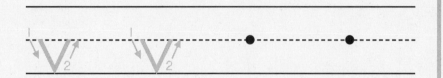

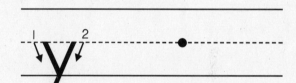

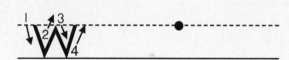

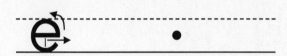

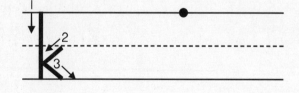

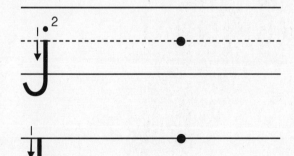

Sentence Page

Sentence Page Lesson 101

Diz can hop.

Name _____

Picture Page

Activity 4

Name _____

Writer's Warm-Up

V V

V V • • | • •

z •   y •

k •   w •

j •   g •

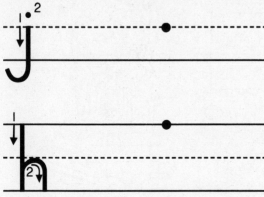
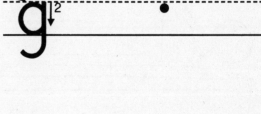

h •

© Pearson Education, Inc.

Silly Words

Name _____

Writer's Warm-Up

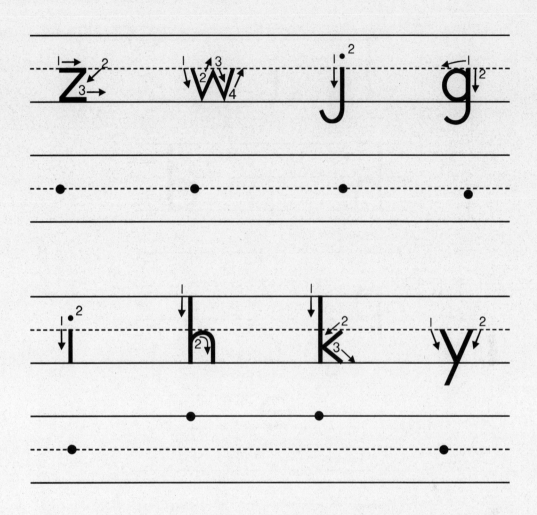

Missing Letters

I   i

h   d

p

e

z   p

d

l

Sentence Page

Sentence Page | Lesson 103

it.

it ?	hit

hit	can

I	I

Can	Yes,

Picture Page

Picture Page Lesson 103

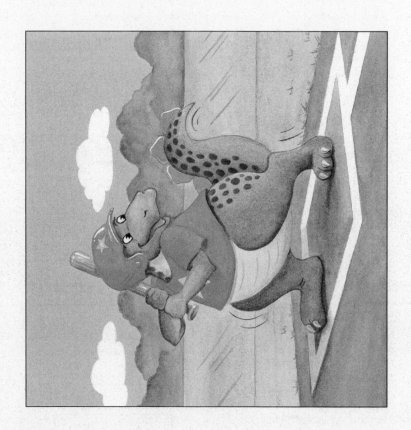

Name _____

Writer's Warm-Up

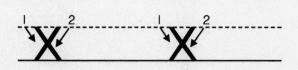

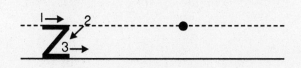

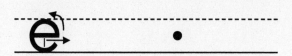

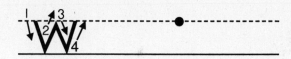

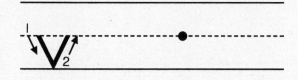

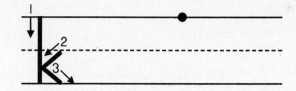

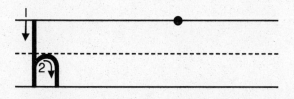

Sentence Page

Sentence Page   Lesson 104

the

in

run

I can

I

sun.

I can

win.

Picture Page

Picture Page

Activity 4

Writer's Warm-Up

x x

x x

z y

e w

v k

h

© Pearson Education, Inc.

Word Writing Game

_____ _____ _____

- - - - - - - - - - - - - - - - - - - -

_____ _____ _____

- - - - - - - - - - - - - - - - - - - -

_____ _____ _____

- - - - - - - - - - - - - - - - - - - -

_____ _____ _____

- - - - - - - - - - - - - - - - - - - -

_____ _____ _____

- - - - - - - - - - - - - - - - - - - -

_____ _____ _____

- - - - - - - - - - - - - - - - - - - -

_____ _____ _____

- - - - - - - - - - - - - - - - - - - -

_____ _____ _____

- - - - - - - - - - - - - - - - - - - -

_____ _____ _____

Treasure Hunt

Name _____

Sentence Page

Sentence Page Lesson 106

The sun was hot.

He got wet.

Name _____

Picture Page

Picture Page Lesson 106

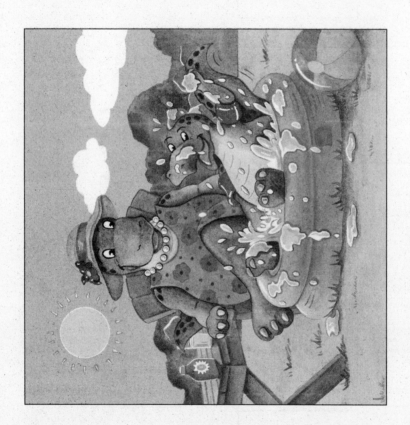

36 Activity 5

Name _____

Writer's Warm-Up

q q

q q • • | • •

z • y •

e • x •

v • k •

h •

Missing Letters

_ _ _

c a _

_ _ _

n _ t

_ _ _

_ _ n

_ _ _

_ i _

_ _ _

m _ n

_ _ _

p _ _

_ _ _

_ e _

Sentence Page | Lesson 107

in.	got	bug	A

fun.	was	It

Name _____

Picture Page

Name _____

Writer's Warm-Up

q   q

q   q   •   • | •   •

z   •   y   •

e   •   x   •

v   •   k   •

h   •

Activity 5
41

Guess What I Am

Writer's Warm-Up

q   •   y   •

x   •   h   •

v   •   z   •

k   •   e   •

r   •   w   •

Sentence Page Lesson 109

Dan can hop in

the big red van.

Activity 3

45

Name _____

Picture Page

Activity 3

46

Letter Mission

Word Maze

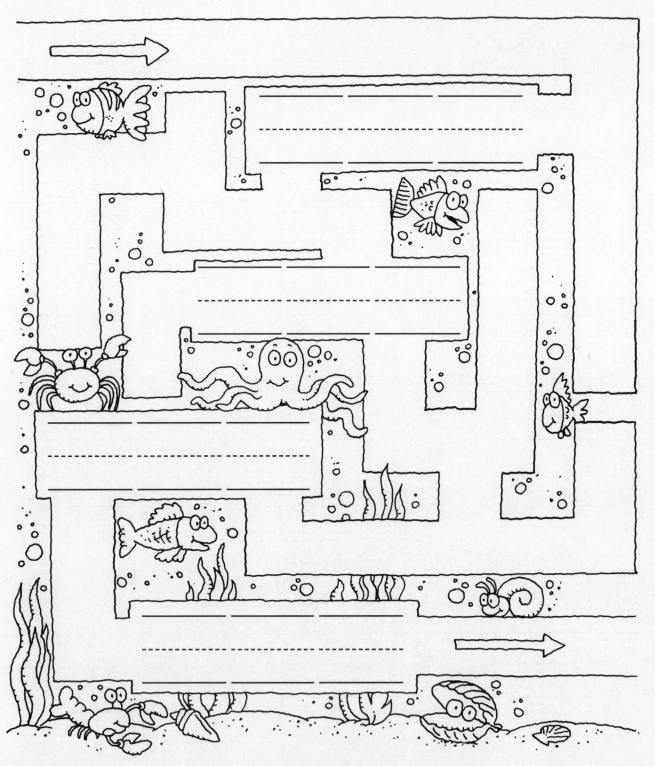

Name _____

Sentence Page

Sentence Page Lesson 110

the

in

Tim

Was

van?

red

big

in

was

he

Yes,

van.

red

big

the.

Picture Page

Picture Page   Lesson 110

Name _____

Writer's Warm-Up

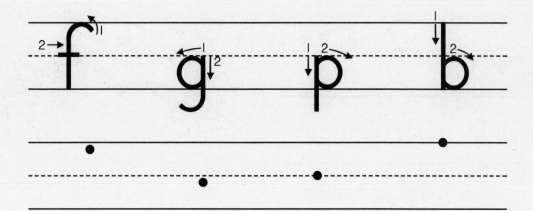

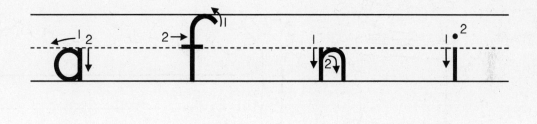

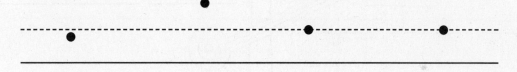

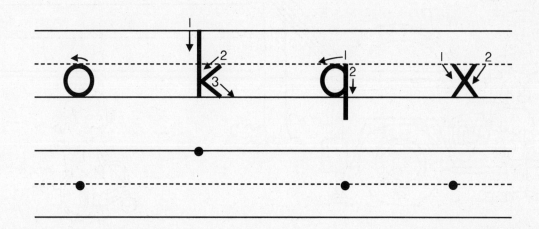

Name _____

Rescue the Cat

_____
- - - - - - - - - - - - - - - -
_____

_____
- - - - - - - - - - - - - - - -

_____
- - - - - - - - - - - - - - - -
_____

_____
- - - - - - - - - - - - - - - -

_____
- - - - - - - - - - - - - - - -

Activity 6

52

Name _____

Sentence Page

Sentence Page　Lesson 112

Diz had a pet pup.

The pup was Bud.

Name _____

Picture Page

Picture Page | Lesson 112

Name _____

Writer's Warm-Up

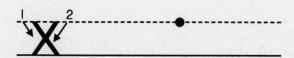

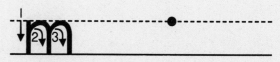

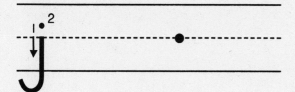

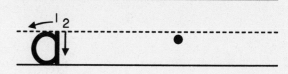

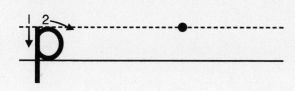

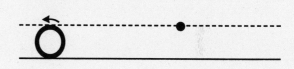

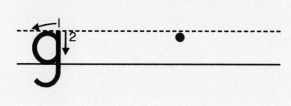

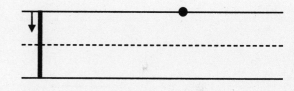

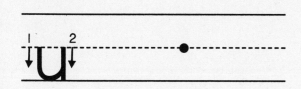

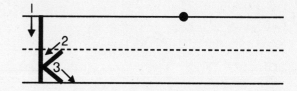

Sentence Page Lesson 113

He fed him.

Diz said, "Run, Bud."

Name _____

Picture Page

Picture Page Lesson 113

Treasure Hunt

Name _____

Silly Words

Name _____

Writer's Warm-Up

z

f

d

b

p

u

n

i

s

e

Activity 4

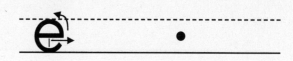

61

Sentence Page — Lesson 115

A pup dug in the mud.

The pup dug up a nut.

Pop! The nut hit a log.

Picture Page

Letter Mission

Sentence Page Lesson 116

Diz sat on the log.

The nut went up.

A nut was in the cup.

Activity 3

67

Name _____

Picture Page

Activity 3

Name _____

Writer's Warm-Up

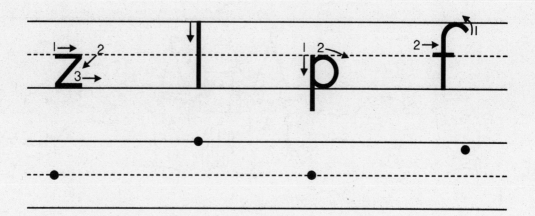

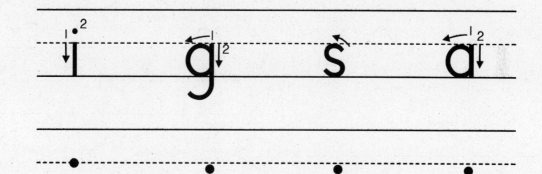

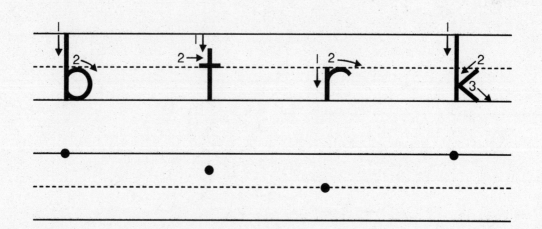

Activity 4

69

Jack and the Beanstalk

Name _____

_____ _____ _____

- -

_____ _____ _____

_____ _____

- - - - - - - - - - - - - - - - - - - -

_____ _____

_____ _____ _____

- -

_____ _____ _____

_____ _____

- - - - - - - - - - - - - - - - - - - -

_____ _____

_____ _____ _____

- -

_____ _____ _____

_____ _____ _____

- -

_____ _____ _____

Sentence Page Lesson 118

Tag is fun!

Tap! Diz is it.

Can Diz tag Max?

Picture Page

Writer's Warm-Up

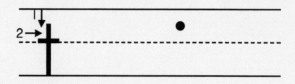

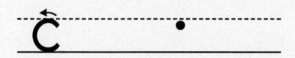

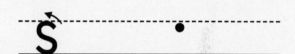

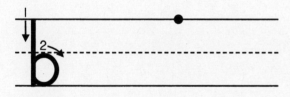

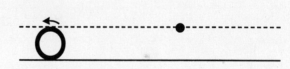

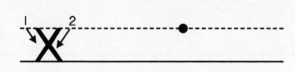

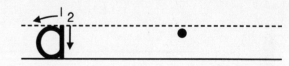

Sentence Page Lesson 119

Diz can not tag Max.

Ron is not fast.

Yes, Pam can tag Ron.

Picture Page

© Pearson Education, Inc.

Treasure Hunt

Activity 4

Name _____

Writer's Warm-Up

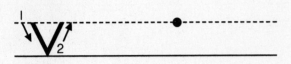

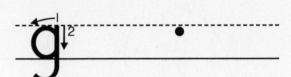

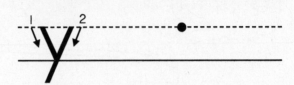

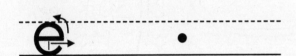

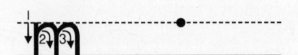

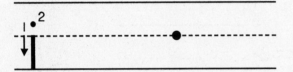

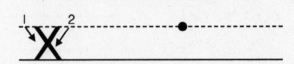

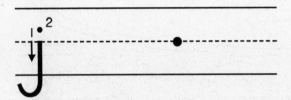

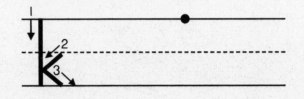

Name _____

Silly Words

Activity 6

Name _____

© Pearson Education, Inc.

Sentence Page | Lesson 121

Diz and Rex set up a box.

Diz got a bun and jam.

Get a bun with jam!

83

Picture Page

Picture Page

Name _____

Letter Mission

Rescue the Cat

_____ _____ _____

- -

_____

_____ _____ _____

- -

_____

_____ _____ _____

- -

_____

_____ _____ _____

- -

_____

Sentence Page Lesson 122

Get ham on a bun!

Jan and Nat had a bun with jam. Yum!

Ted and Ben had ham on a bun. Yum!

Picture Page

Picture Page Lesson 122

Name _____

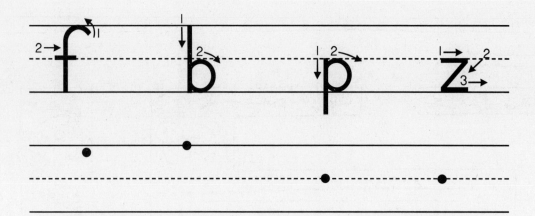

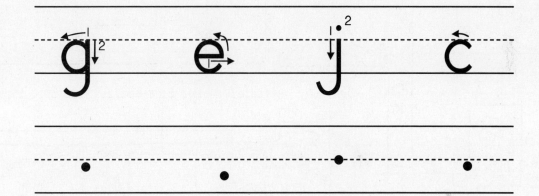

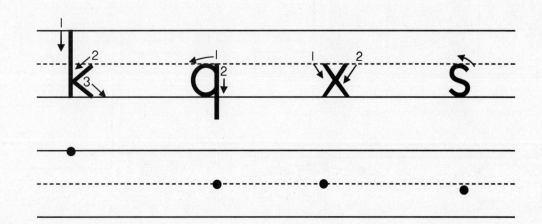

Word Maze

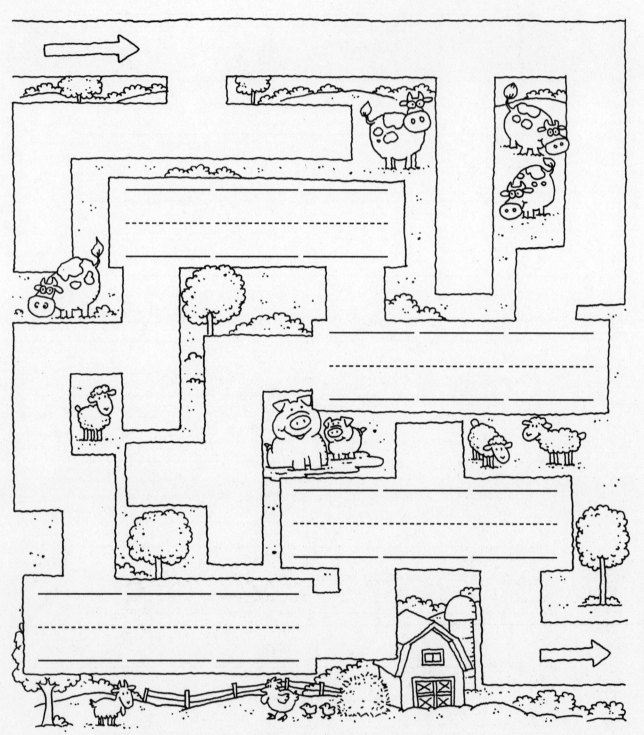

Activity 6

Name _____

Sentence Page (Lesson 124)

Diz and Sam sat in the sand.

Sam had a net.

Diz had a big cup with a lid.

Name _____

Picture Page

Name _____

Writer's Warm-Up

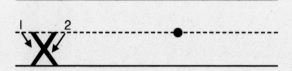

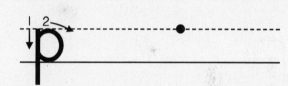

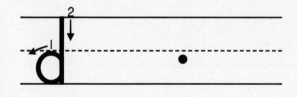

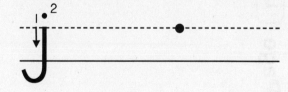

Sentence Page

Sentence Page | Lesson 125

Sam said to get up fast!

A big bug was on top of Diz.

Will Diz get the bug with the cup?

Name _____

Picture Page

Activity 3

Name _____

Treasure Hunt

Word Writing Game

_____ _____ _____

_____ _____ _____

_____ _____ _____

_____ _____ _____

_____ _____ _____

_____ _____ _____

_____ _____ _____

_____ _____ _____

_____ _____ _____

_____ _____ _____

Writer's Warm-Up

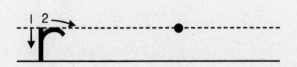

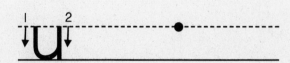

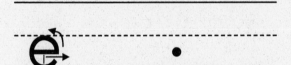

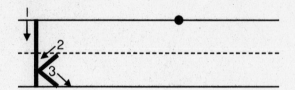

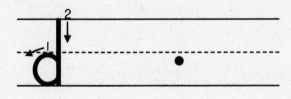

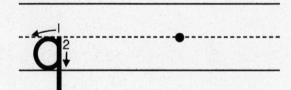

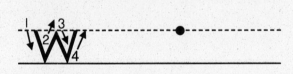

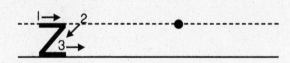

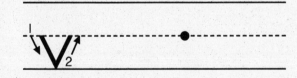

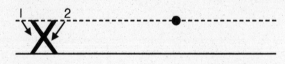